Ellis Island

by Lori Mortensen

illustrated by Matthew Skeens

PICTURE WINDOW BOOKS
Minneapolis, Minnesota

Special thanks to our advisers for their expertise:

Jeffrey S. Dosik, Librarian Technician, National Park Service
Statue of Liberty National Monument and Ellis Island

Terry Flaherty, Ph.D., Professor of English
Minnesota State University, Mankato

Editor: Shelly Lyons
Designers: Abbey Fitzgerald
Page Production: Melissa Kes
Art Director: Nathan Gassman
Associate Managing Editor: Christianne Jones
The illustrations in this book were created digitally.
Photo Credit: Shutterstock/ifoto, 23

Picture Window Books
151 Good Counsel Drive
P.O. Box 669
Mankato, MN 56002-0669
877-845-8392\
www.picturewindowbooks.com

All books published by Picture Window Books
are manufactured with paper containing at least
10 percent post-consumer waste.

Library of Congress Cataloging-in-Publication Data
Mortensen, Lori, 1955-
Ellis Island / by Lori Mortensen ; illustrated by Matthew Skeens.
p. cm. — (American symbols)
Includes index.
ISBN 978-1-4048-4705-7 (library binding)
1. Ellis Island Immigration Station (N.Y. and N.J.)—History—Juvenile
literature. 2. Immigrants—United States—History—Juvenile literature.
3. United States—Emigration and immigration—History—Juvenile literature.
I. Skeens, Matthew, ill. II. Title.
JV6484.M675 2008
304.8'73—dc22   2008006341

Table of Contents

Welcome to Ellis Island! My name is Sophie. My grandparents first came to the United States through Ellis Island in New York. Ellis Island is an important symbol of freedom in the United States. I will tell you why.

Journey to Freedom

During the 1800s, people in Europe faced many hardships. War, hunger, and unfair laws made it difficult for families to survive. To escape these problems, people left Europe and came to the United States. For them, the United States was the land of hope, opportunity, and the "American Dream."

By 1892, millions of people were sailing to the United States. Many of them arrived at Ellis Island. It became the gateway to freedom—and a new life in the United States.

People came to the United States from many countries, including England, Ireland, Italy, France, Finland, and Russia.

A Safe Place

Thousands of immigrants began arriving at Ellis Island each day. The government decided to build an immigration center on Ellis Island. The center would be a safe place for immigrants to arrive in the United States. Medical inspectors would check immigrants for disease. Inspectors would decide who could live in the United States and who could not.

Hundreds of immigrants sailed in crowded ships for up to two weeks at a time. They often traveled in the ship's steerage—the bottom of the ship. Steerage was crowded, smelly, and noisy.

A Grand Opening

The Ellis Island Immigration Center opened on January 1, 1892. It had a large main building, a dining area, a kitchen, and a place where people could sleep.

In 1993, Ireland and the United States honored Annie Moore and her historic journey with two statues. One statue is located at Cobh, Ireland, the seaport where Annie began her journey. The other statue is at Ellis Island.

Annie Moore, an Irish girl, was the first person to go through Ellis Island. In honor of the grand event, officials gave her a $10 gold piece. It was a special surprise, because it was Annie's 15th birthday, too.

A Long Wait

It usually took three to five hours for an immigrant to be processed at Ellis Island. Being processed meant going through a medical inspection and then questioning.

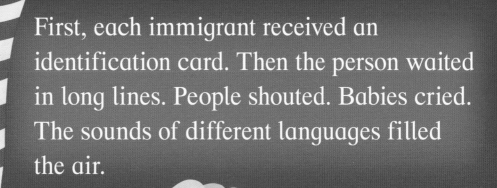

First, each immigrant received an identification card. Then the person waited in long lines. People shouted. Babies cried. The sounds of different languages filled the air.

Ellis Island was designed to process 5,000 people a day. But sometimes, twice as many immigrants arrived. The record was set on April 17, 1907, when 11,747 people were processed.

Medical Exam

Medical inspectors checked immigrants for more than 50 different diseases and conditions. Some of the diseases included eye infections, measles, and mumps.

People who could get well were treated at the hospital. People who could not be cured were forced to return to their homeland.

To process immigrants faster, inspectors used chalk to mark the coats of those who were ill. Letters stood for health problems. For example, the letter *E* stood for "eye disease."

Ticket to Freedom

An immigrant who passed the medical inspection went on to the Registry Room. There, another inspector asked the person about family members in the United States, whether the person had money, and whether the person had a police record. The immigrant's answers helped the inspector decide whether he or she would be a good citizen.

An immigrant who passed the questioning received a landing card. It was a ticket to freedom and a new life in the United States.

Most immigrants did not speak English. Inspectors used interpreters to communicate with immigrants who spoke a different language.

On June 14, 1897, a fire broke out in the Ellis Island Immigration Center's kitchen. It quickly spread and burned all of the wooden buildings to the ground. The immigration center was destroyed.

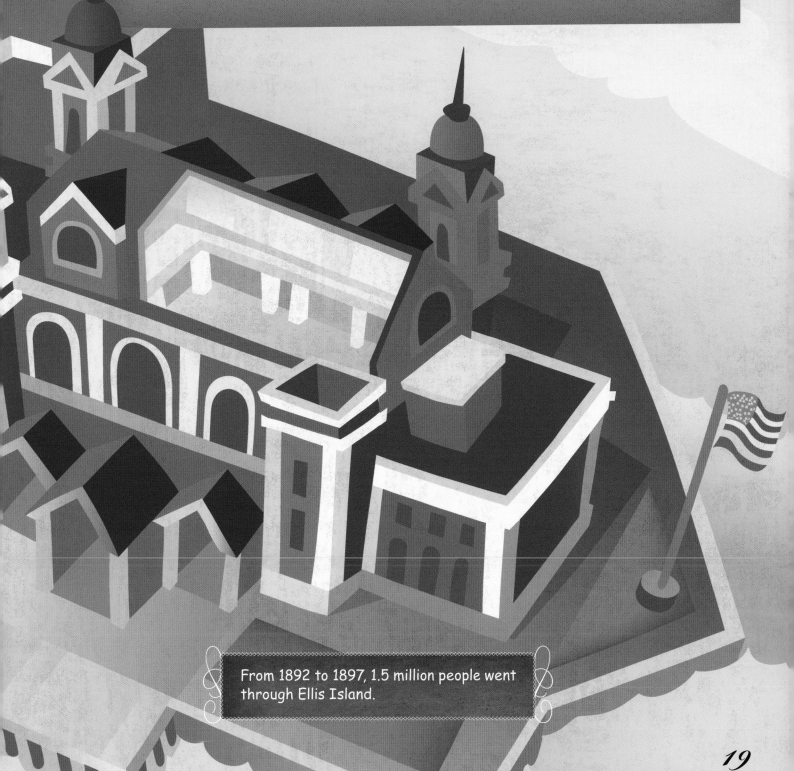

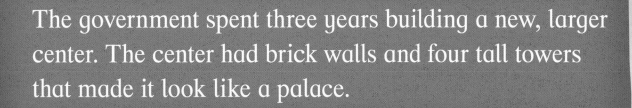

The government spent three years building a new, larger center. The center had brick walls and four tall towers that made it look like a palace.

From 1892 to 1897, 1.5 million people went through Ellis Island.

19

Closing Ellis Island's Doors

In 1924, President Coolidge signed the Immigration Act of 1924. The act said people should pass an immigration inspection at a U.S. embassy in their home country before they sailed to the United States. This greatly reduced the number of immigrants coming into the United States.

When Ellis Island's immigration center was no longer needed, the government used it for other things. During World War II (1939-1945), it was a detention center.

In 1954, government officials closed Ellis Island's doors. Upkeep of the buildings had become too costly. By then, more than 12 million immigrants had come through Ellis Island.

The millions of immigrants who passed through the immigration center never forgot Ellis Island and what it represented—freedom to make a new life.

Today the Ellis Island Immigration Museum is a treasured gateway to our country's past. It is a symbol of freedom. It honors the immigrants, like my grandparents, who sailed to the United States searching for the "American Dream."

I hope you enjoyed your visit. Come again soon. Everyone is welcome!

Ellis Island Facts

Ellis Island

- Throughout the years, the U.S. government had workers enlarge Ellis Island with dirt from the digging of subway tunnels. The island grew from 3.3 acres (1.3 hectares) to almost 27.5 acres (11 ha).

- Twelve million people passed through Ellis Island. About 2 percent, or about 250,000 people, were forced to return to their homeland. Because of this, Ellis Island was also known as the "Island of Tears."

- Forty to 50 percent of the people living in the United States today could trace their family to an Ellis Island immigrant.

- In 1990, Ellis Island officials unveiled the Wall of Honor, the largest wall of names in the world. Thousands of names are engraved on the wall to honor the heritage of U.S. families.

- In 1965, President Lyndon B. Johnson made Ellis Island part of the Statue of Liberty Monument. The Statue of Liberty is located on an island near Ellis Island.

Glossary

citizen — someone who has the right to live in a country

embassy — a place where representatives of a foreign country live and work

hardship — something that causes suffering; usually war, hunger, and poverty

immigrant — a person who leaves one country and settles in another

inspection — the process of looking over or reviewing something

interpreter — a person who hears one language and translates its meaning into another

steerage — the least expensive place for passengers to travel in a ship; it was called steerage because it was located near the rudder (the rudder helped steer the ship)

To Learn More

More Books to Read

DeGezelle, Terry. *Ellis Island*. Mankato, Minn.: Capstone Press, 2006.

Landau, Elaine. *Ellis Island*. New York: Children's Press, 2008.

Peacock, Louise. *At Ellis Island: A History in Many Voices*. New York: Atheneum Books, 2007.

Sandler, Martin W. *Island of Hope: The Story of Ellis Island and the Journey to America*. New York: Scholastic, 2004.

On the Web

FactHound offers a safe, fun way to find Web sites related to topics in this book. All of the sites on FactHound have been researched by our staff.

1. Visit *www.facthound.com*
2. Type in this special code: 1404847057
3. Click on the FETCH IT button.

Your trusty FactHound will fetch the best sites for you!

Index

Look for all of the books in the American Symbols series:

Angel Island
The Bald Eagle
The Bill of Rights
Ellis Island
The Great Seal of the United States

The Liberty Bell
The Lincoln Memorial
Our American Flag
Our National Anthem
Our U.S. Capitol
The Pledge of Allegiance

The Statue of Liberty
Uncle Sam
The U.S. Constitution
The U.S. Supreme Court
The White House

24